COMFORTING MYTHS

Concerning the Political in Art

RABIH ALAMEDDINE

University of Virginia Press
CHARLOTTESVILLE AND LONDON

The University of Virginia Press is situated on the traditional lands of the Monacan Nation, and the Commonwealth of Virginia was and is home to many other Indigenous people. We pay our respect to all of them, past and present. We also honor the enslaved African and African American people who built the University of Virginia, and we recognize their descendants. We commit to fostering voices from these communities through our publications and to deepening our collective understanding of their histories and contributions.

University of Virginia Press
© 2024 by Rabih Alameddine
All rights reserved
Printed in the United States of America on acid-free paper
First published 2024

9 8 7 6 5 4 3 2 1

LIBRARY OF CONGRESS CATALOGING-IN-PUBLICATION DATA

Names: Alameddine, Rabih, author.
Title: Comforting myths : concerning the political in art / Rabih Alameddine.
Description: Charlottesville : University of Virginia Press, 2024. | Series: Kapnick foundation distinguished writer-in-residence lectures
Identifiers: LCCN 2024016350 (print) | LCCN 2024016351 (ebook) | ISBN 9780813952512 (hardcover) | ISBN 9780813952529 (ebook)
Subjects: LCSH: Fiction—History and criticism. | Politics in literature. | Politics and literature. | Arts—Political aspects. | BISAC: LANGUAGE ARTS & DISCIPLINES / Writing / Fiction Writing | LITERARY CRITICISM / Subjects & Themes / Culture, Race & Ethnicity | LCGFT: Essays.
Classification: LCC PN3491 .A43 2024 (print) | LCC PN3491 (ebook) | DDC 809.3—dc23/eng/20240416
LC record available at https://lccn.loc.gov/2024016350
LC ebook record available at https://lccn.loc.gov/2024016351

Cover design: David Drummond

For Randa

CONTENTS

Concerning the Political in Art

1

Comforting Myths: Notes from a Purveyor

45

Afterword:
He's Angry about All the Right Things

Joumana Khatib

69

Acknowledgments

81

COMFORTING MYTHS

CONCERNING THE
POLITICAL IN ART

Every time I talk politics in this country, I notice that people's faces go blank. Never fails. I come from Lebanon, a culture where citizens not only talk politics, they never shut up. It's a national obsession. Over here, we have talk shows with Oprah or Ellen, stars with only first names talking to celebrities. In Lebanon, there are three-hour talk shows about what the government is doing, or whether what happened in Tel Aviv, Tehran, or Riyadh would affect the price of wheat in Beirut. Over here, good manners suggest that you not bring up politics at a dinner party. In Lebanon, that would be considered a terrible dinner party. If there are not two or three major political arguments, maybe a flying plate or two, the dinner might be considered boring.

Now, I might be exaggerating, and of course I'm generalizing. There are Lebanese who don't care about politics and many Americans who do. The situation has changed quite a bit these days, but when I first arrived in this country and for a long time thereafter, politics was thought of as tedious. If two people were talking and one uttered the word *political*, the other nodded off, almost a Pavlovian response.

Let's call the symptom politico-narcolepsy.

So, of course, I decide to give a talk on the political in literature.

For as long as I can remember, I've been told that political novels are bad novels—or at least, not very good. Even back in high school, in Lebanon, our English teacher, a lovely man hailing all the way from New Zealand, explained to us, his less than eager students, that political literature is not very good because it's didactic. That did not mean that we shouldn't read it; after all, *Animal Farm* was on the syllabus that year, if I remember correctly. Political works serve a purpose and can benefit society in various ways, he said. But if we wanted to read literature, with a capital *L,* this ephemeral thing that moved not just minds but souls and mountains, we should look for writers like Shakespeare, whose writing was artistic and not political.

I was fourteen or fifteen at the time. Yet even then I had an inkling that his position was tenuous at best, or to put it in words I would have used at the time, *such bullshit.* I knew it was even though I was yet to read any of Shakespeare's history plays. I don't think any sane man would ever suggest *Richard III* or *Henry V* aren't political, or *Julius Caesar,* or *Macbeth* for that matter. But that year we were reading *Romeo and Juliet,* a love story, which according to our teacher wasn't political. I am Lebanese, so of course I saw it as political. Romeo and Juliet belonged to two families who couldn't stand each other, who wouldn't speak to each other. We had families like that in the mountain village I came from. Some people in the village voted for the Jumblatt family in every election and the others voted for the Arslan family. Even though the entire village was of the same sect, mostly the same class, what clan they belonged to and who they were loyal to determined everything. I saw the play as political.

I would encounter that argument—that if a novel is political, it is less than, that it could never be as good as a literary novel—all through my life as a writer, particularly here in the US. That position was promulgated by many an established writer, by quite a few literary magazines and journals, and across the board in MFA programs. What was not always stated outright, though usually an underlying assumption, is that political novels are not literary, that literature should rise above the pettiness of politics, that art should be separate from politics. I have heard it said many a time, "The province of art is the human condition." Writing about the human condition is the only subject a literary writer should deal with.

I have said in interviews, on panels, screamed it from rooftops, so I will say it here once more: Writing about the human condition is a political act; in fact, it might be one of the greatest political acts.

In 2016 I attended the Association of Writers and Writing Programs Conference in Los Angeles. I must admit here that I'm not a big fan of conferences in general—I don't do well in large crowds; it's not exactly a phobia, but it's close enough—and I'm not fond of writing conferences in particular. As an aside, I remember attending the Jaipur Literature Festival, which I believe is the biggest lit fest of them all. On my first day, I walked by a group of festival volunteers as they were being trained, and the trainer was standing in front of the group explaining loudly what they should do in case of a stampede. I spent three days freaking out. I mean, they have four million attendees and I'm just one person. A stampede? I still shudder just thinking about it. I mention this to point out that I feel anxious at festivals, which is why I might not always be that diplomatic when I'm there.

In any case, I attended the AWP conference, and I wasn't exactly happy about it. I was booked on a panel called "Politics and Literary Fiction." Now, I do consider my work to be political, so I wasn't exactly shocked to be chosen for that panel, but I was promoting my novel *An Unnecessary Woman,* about a reclusive seventy-two-year-old woman who translates literary books that no one reads and who hardly leaves her apartment. It might be the least overtly political of all my novels, yet here I was on the panel with, mind you, two other hyphenated Americans and a Brit. I might not have been shocked, but I was, shall we say, a bit weirded out. It was a large audience. And then I began to notice during the Q&A that the reason *An Unnecessary Woman* was considered political was because it was set in Beirut, because, you know, I was commenting on the plight of women in a terribly patriarchal country. Had I placed the novel in NYC or Houston and kept the same themes, it wouldn't be political, because, you know, we don't really live in a patriarchal culture here. So I slowly became less "weirded out" and returned to my natural state: grumpy. I couldn't believe what I was hearing. Many of the questions from the audience veered into "literature shouldn't be political," my pet peeve, and I told the audience off. I said, "The only way you can think that politics is separate from literature is if the political system is working for you."

There, I said it.

Again.

Maybe I should have said it more diplomatically.

I must have said a few things that were undiplomatic. The friends who were in the audience said something about blanched faces and horrified gasps. I blame my anxiety, which is exacerbated by writing conferences.

Now, of course, things have changed since I started writing a couple of decades ago and changed drastically since I was in high school in

Lebanon. People seem to be able to talk politics these days—some won't shut up about it. I guess we're becoming more Lebanese. Political novels are more common, so common in fact that we might even call it a genre. A friend of mine suggests that writers these days are indoctrinated with the opposite of what I was: that being "political" is of the utmost importance. He loves to say that art simply isn't very good at politics—if an artist wants to make a difference, they should go into actual politics. Putting aside for a moment whether writing could be an effective tool for change, he is right that we seem to praise political writing more these days, particularly writings that deal with what we call identity politics.

I'd heard that two poets serving on the jury for the National Book Award recently were having a discussion in which one poet strongly supported a book and the other opposed it. The latter did not appreciate poems dealing with aesthetics: beautiful poems did not move her; political poems did. Now, I think that's an inordinately stupid comment, as if the beautiful and the political are at different ends of a spectrum. Just stupid. A poet who doesn't appreciate beauty makes no sense to me. Aesthetics is my bread and butter—beauty is all the food groups and ice cream too. But let me take the statement that what's beautiful is inherently not political a bit further. Suppose we have a poem about a blooming flower, how gorgeously the petals unfurl, how the play of light affects said unfurling. The poet who hates beautiful poems might tell us that this isn't a political poem. But what if it is read by a woman in, say, Lubbock, Texas, who sees the poem as a metaphor for claiming one's power? Say she decides to enroll in a community college, gets her real estate license, leaves her good-for-nothing husband, and starts her own company. Can we now consider the flower poem political? What if it is read by a young gay boy who sees it as a metaphor for transformation and growing? He comes out of the closet and, I don't know, starts a local gay rights group in Milledgeville, Georgia, or some village in Jordan. Is the flower poem political?

This is the old intent-versus-interpretation argument. We usually assume that it is the intent of the poem that determines whether it is political or not. I'm not sure that's the case. My work might be political, but when I sit down to write, politics is rarely on my mind. My intent isn't political, at least not overtly so. Like most writers, I'm worried about how to make a sentence work, how to move from one paragraph to the next, how to make the story flow, how to bring the characters to life. I can't tell you the intent of the writer of the flower poem—particularly since we just made her up. I can only look at the result, and for me, a work of art doesn't exist without a receiver: viewer or reader. A painting is just an object if no one sees it, but it becomes a painting or a work of art when seen. Does a novel exist without a reader, a reader who is the novel's interpreter? A book is just a book.

Can how a book is read make it political?

One of the great novels of our time is Bulgakov's *The Master and Margarita,* a magical, satirical dark comedy that defies categorization. It was banned in the Soviet Union and caused its writer all kinds of problems. Now, the actual story, a devil visiting a small town in Russia, is not overtly political. Allegorically, it's a devastating attack on the governing powers. A number of novels written under criminally repressive regimes do the same. I understand that most likely, Bulgakov's intent was to write a political novel, but how can we be sure of that when we read it? If his intent was only to write a beautiful novel, would it still be so?

Can how a book is read make it political?

On the other hand, since I as a writer have little control as to how my work is interpreted, I desperately want to believe that my intent is what matters.

I find it difficult to unspool the threads of intent/interpretation arguments.

What I would like to unspool is why we seem to consider political writing to be separate from the literary kind, or in the case of the silly poet, why political and beautiful must oppose each other. When I was thinking about this talk, I asked various friends what they considered a political novel and what they thought was not. Their replies were enlightening. A French friend, Philippe, said he disliked political novels. He then added, "*The Count of Monte Cristo* is the most savage attack on France's 1840s social, judicial, and political system that I can think of. But is it a 'political novel'? No."

I found that curious. How could a novel that attacks a political system be considered apolitical? The answer to that seems to be that for many people, a novel that's political has to be overtly so, where the message overpowers everything. Philippe made sure to explain to me that my novels were not political, even though I certainly thought they were.

The subject also came up in a conversation I was having with the magnificent Australian writer Richard Flanagan in a dowdy bar in Adelaide of all places. I'm paraphrasing here, but Richard suggested that writers need not concern themselves with politics—that our ideal is to emulate Franz Kafka: lock ourselves in a room and write whatever moves us. I agree with that sentiment, of course, but had he said Proust instead of Kafka, it would have made more sense to me. I mean, really, I consider Kafka one of our great writers, and his work is certainly most political. What is stranger is that Flanagan's novels are all astounding and are unequivocally political. His novel *Gould's Book of Fish* is about a convict who falls in love with a Black woman and tells the history of Australia's conception. His Booker Prize–winning novel *The Narrow Road to the Deep North* is the story of the Death Railway, which was built by Japanese war camp prisoners. Hell, he has a novel titled *The Unknown Terrorist.*

Basically, many don't consider his work to be political because his novels deal with more than just politics, or to use the more common term, "rise above" politics. The characters are well developed, the plots gripping, and the language exquisite. I consider them very much so, obviously.

Does any book rise above politics? Here's a quote from probably the most well-known political writer, George Orwell: "In our age there is no such thing as 'keeping out of politics.' All issues are political issues, and politics itself is a mass of lies, evasions, folly, hatred, and schizophrenia."

COMFORTING MYTHS

For as long as I can remember, manifestly political novels have always aroused some degree of suspicion. Milan Kundera once dismissed Orwell's *Nineteen Eighty-Four* as "political thought disguised as a novel." In a devastating review, Whittaker Chambers said that Ayn Rand's colossal and interminable *Atlas Shrugged* "can be called a novel only by devaluing the term. . . . Its story merely serves Miss Rand to get the customers inside the tent, and as a soapbox for delivering her Message." Message with a capital *M*.

Until a few years ago, the mantra that great art is not political was de rigueur. Yet the examples offered as political novels were always patently bad novels, where the political agenda overpowered everything in the book. I mean, *Atlas Shrugged?* Really? That one is such an awful novel by any standard. Its agenda is so blatant, and blatantly idiotic. As an aside, I've had at least one person tell me that it might not be a good novel, but he had learned a lot from its philosophy. Anyone who claims that

CONCERNING THE POLITICAL IN ART

Rand has a philosophy has not read philosophy. The philosophy of Pee-wee Herman is more rigorous and disciplined than that of Ayn Rand. "I know you are but what am I?"

As much as I like Orwell's *Nineteen Eighty-Four* and *Animal Farm,* they're not good novels.

Basically, the examples offered as political novels are always agenda-driven ones, books that proselytize, that lack subtlety. It's not a coincidence that the majority of Ayn Rand's fans are boys who came across her work as teenagers, when furious hormones drive away any hint of subtlety. Are agenda-driven novels always bad? Well, I'm not a fan. I think most novels that hit you over the head with a two-by-four are not very good. That's not to say they can't be effective, even necessary at times. *The Jungle,* Upton Sinclair's horrific exposé of the plight of immigrant workers in the Chicago meatpacking industry, prompted Theodore Roosevelt to establish the forerunner of the Food and Drug Administration. Is *The Jungle* a good novel? I loved it when I read it as a young man, and it certainly was effective, but I don't think it's very good. There are many other examples of manifestly political novels that weren't very good but were effective at proselytizing. Harriet Beecher Stowe's *Uncle Tom's Cabin* fired up the abolitionist movement.

Again, I'd like you to notice that even when we're talking about campaigning political novels, nobody offers as examples the truly great ones, those that proselytize and are magnificent. Chinua Achebe's anticolonialist masterpiece *Things Fall Apart* or Aleksandr Solzhenitsyn's gulag chronicle *One Day in the Life of Ivan Denisovich.* For many, one of literature's most famous works of fiction, Joseph Conrad's *Heart of Darkness,* isn't considered political despite its total lack of subtlety in its political message.

So it seems that for many critics, a great political novel isn't political and a bad one is.

A political novel can only be bad.

CONCERNING THE POLITICAL IN ART

Now, most novels have themes rather than an agenda, and usually more than just one. Yet for many readers, political themes are glossed over. And there are many reasons for this, including some that, in my opinion, go directly to the heart of problems of this country we live in.

Once when he was accepting an award in an Eastern European city, Philip Roth told the audience—and I'm paraphrasing here again since unfortunately I've been unable to find the exact quote—that as strange as it might sound, he envied Eastern European writers because the act of writing seemed more urgent for them, a matter of life and death at times. I know he didn't mean that he'd be willing to change places with writers living under censorship, severe repression, and murderous dictatorships. I know he didn't mean that we should torture writers in order to make them write better novels (though I've thought about torturing writing students quite often).

I assume Philip Roth believed that writing under horrific conditions forced writers to be more creative, their work becoming imperative and indispensable. I wholeheartedly agree with him. Many of my favorite writers are Eastern Europeans, and South Americans, or Africans—writers who lived under restrictive or dangerous governments. It is true that there's an urgency to their work. What I find troublesome is the inference that for American writers, life is easier and more comfortable, so our work reflects that.

The problem, and I hope this is something that we all understand these days, is that life is more comfortable for some Americans, not for all of us. As an Arab living in this country, my life is certainly not easier. For an African American who constantly worries about being shot at on a whim, life is not some piece of cake. For minorities, for immigrants, for queers, for all those on the margins of the dominant culture, for those living below the poverty line, life isn't always comfortable.

When writers belonging to the margins of the dominant culture write about their daily lives, what it is like for them to live in their country, their work is considered political.

CONCERNING THE POLITICAL IN ART

When writers belonging in the center of the dominant culture write about their daily lives, what it is like for them to live in their country, their work is considered not political.

Again, I do agree with Roth. I think African American writers, immigrants, queers, Asian Americans, and Latinos are writing novels that are urgent and important because, let's face it, lives are more at stake. Many have more skin in the game, so to speak. And yes, that work is political as well.

What I would like to state here is that novels by writers who are part of the dominant culture are political as well. As George Orwell wrote, "No book is genuinely free from political bias. The opinion that art should have nothing to do with politics is itself a political attitude."

Let me give an example. If your country is raining bombs on another country and you choose to write about a couple getting a divorce in Minneapolis, that's a political decision. This doesn't mean the novel would be good or bad, urgent or not. I'm just saying it's a political decision. If you write about a stockbroker trying to make peace with his children while your government is placing immigrant children in cages, that's a political attitude.

Some writers would say that the act of writing is in and of itself a political act, so of course the choice of what to write about falls into that category, but the content, they say, doesn't have to be so.

Now, I'm not sure I can say that every novel is political, but most of what is considered not is.

Let's look at some classics. There are some, not many, who consider Dickens a political writer. His novels use character and narrative to draw the reader's attention to some social ill and to galvanize efforts to remedy it. Very few would consider Jane Austen a political writer even though her novels use character and narrative to draw the reader's attention to some social ill and to galvanize efforts to remedy it. Yes, it's true, Austen is more subtle than Dickens, which is why I prefer her work, but the main reason she's not considered political is because she's writing about the gentry, those who are part of the dominant culture, and Dickens is writing about poor people, who are not.

Neither Austen nor Dickens writes agenda-driven novels, but that doesn't make their work any less political. Jane Austen disturbs the pretensions of England's dominant culture with the best of them. She does it with delicacy and subtlety, but she does it nonetheless. Her novels are political, just like Dickens's, just like, say, Voltaire's. Austen wanted to change her culture. She was a revolutionary.

Why is it so difficult for us to see her and her work as political?

Tim O'Brien's novel *The Things They Carried* deals with the experience of American soldiers in Vietnam. It is critical of the Vietnam War and considered a political novel. John Updike supported the war in Indochina. I haven't read all of his novels, but I don't remember him writing about the effect of Vietnam on his characters, on the communities he wrote about. If your country is blanket bombing another, if an entire generation of its young men are killing and being killed, or being traumatized in a foreign country, and the novel you're writing is set in an idyllic suburbia, with the book's narrative tension a husband considering cheating on his wife, how is that not a political novel?

How is a novel that exalts a way of life, any way of life, not political?

A novel about a doctor who moves to a small town and is beaten up by drunks upon arrival is considered not, but an immigrant who moves to a small town and gets attacked is.

Let me state this clearly: If a novel reinforces the dominant society's values, that culture will not think of the novel as political; if it doesn't, it will. If a novel threatens how the dominant culture views itself, the dominant culture considers it political.

Now, please, I don't want to suggest that we should tell writers what to write and what not to. Just because Updike writes about stultifying suburbia doesn't necessarily make his work less interesting or less valuable. I certainly would not want him to write about things that do not interest him just because it might be more urgent. For example,

CONCERNING THE POLITICAL IN ART

I would not want him to write a novel about an eighteen-year-old Egyptian American boy and call it *Terrorist.* I mean, I would support his right to do so, but I would not want him to.

A novelist can write about anything, and it can be urgent, it can be brilliant, and most likely, it is also political.

I don't have to tell you that the level of political discourse in the United States has dropped off dramatically. If a political thought or position cannot be stated in one tweet, it can no longer exist. We shout at each other across various social media platforms and consider that the apex of policy. I would like to suggest that political discourse in our country has been disintegrating for quite a while. I believe this helps those in power.

What has also been apparent to me is how often the abstract noun *politics* and the adjective *political* are used pejoratively. We talk about people playing politics—calling someone political is akin to saying they're a snake. Whenever the Supreme Court comes out with a decision that some faction doesn't like, the response is usually, "When did the court become so political?" For the record, the court has always been political; politics is its reason for being. *Politics* and *political* mean different things to different people, and for most of us, we rarely use these words in a positive way.

I won't talk here about how the limiting of meaning of these words helps the powerful remain in power. I'll leave that to your imagination. What I'm interested in is this teeny tiny piece of our world we call literature: how the fact that we think of politics as somehow detrimental to art is limiting our literature, and how so few of us can agree on what constitutes a political novel.

As I said, in preparation for this talk, I asked a number of friends some questions—I'm a writer, not an academic; my research consists of talking to friends. When I do really deep research, I include acquaintances. When I want research that's outside the box, I talk to my crazy cousin in Beirut.

CONCERNING THE POLITICAL IN ART

I asked my friends: Do you think political novels in general are bad, and if so, why? What makes a novel political and another not? Can art and politics be separated, and if so, should they be?

For the most part, most agreed that political novels are bad, that a novel is political when the message is heavy-handed. I wasn't surprised that quite a few considered novels like *The Handmaid's Tale* and *Fahrenheit 451* not political, or as one friend noted, not very political, even though they boast a strong message or, dare I say, a heavy-handed message. The explanation given was that the novels offer more than just a message, as my friend Philippe said about *The Count of Monte Cristo*.

This might sound reasonable on the surface, but we all know that only atrocious novels offer just a message. Any novel worth its salt interweaves many themes and engages readers on different levels. What most of my friends seemed to be saying is, "If I liked a novel, then it isn't political, but if I didn't, it is."

COMFORTING MYTHS

I consider most novels to be political because I think politics happens organically in human social systems, from the family up. Humans are inherently political in their interactions. Therefore, writing about the human condition is political.

I do understand that my definition of the word *political* is so broad that the word could in essence become meaningless. But I find how our culture defines the word to be so limited that it renders it meaningless as well. Let's consider for a moment the hot topic du jour, identity-based political literature, and what is defined as such.

If I write a novel about an Arab family living in the US, going about their daily lives, loving and hating each other, and so forth, would it be considered identity based? Would it depend on whether I included an incidence or two of discrimination? What if my family were Chinese? What if it were white? As I mentioned earlier, the label of political is tied to perceived threats to how the dominant culture views itself.

CONCERNING THE POLITICAL IN ART

If Colson Whitehead writes a novel about a Black man's life, is it identity politics?

If John Updike writes a novel about a white man's life, is it not identity politics?

On the *New York Times Book Review* podcast recently, the writer Thomas Mallon and the paper's book editor, Pamela Paul, discussed Jonathan Franzen's latest novel, expressing gratitude for the way Franzen keeps politics out of his fiction. Two things quickly came to mind: One, why is keeping politics out of fiction either good or bad; and more troublesome, how is writing about all white characters not by definition identity-based politics?

One of my all-time favorite writers is Alice Munro, whose short stories are miraculous at times. She's Canadian, and the characters in her stories are almost exclusively white and hardly ever encounter any other kind of Canadians. When your country is multiethnic, and has been since its inception, and you ignore every other race, how is that not identity-based political fiction? When she writes about a poor woman from the country struggling in a big city where others are indulging in a never-ending capitalist orgy, how is that not political? Yet when she won the Nobel Prize, a writer friend was ecstatic. "Finally," she said. "The Nobel is recognizing a nonpolitical writer."

Alice Munro writes great literature, and it is political.

In his review of the novel *John Henry Days*, John Updike praised the young Colson Whitehead, particularly his first novel *The Intuitionist*, but then added a comment that boggled my mind. He said that the central character of the novel behaves like any regular white man, so why does he have to be Black? The exact quote is, "The central character . . . need not be black at all. His discontent might just as well be that of a young white or Asian-American of literary bent. [His] educational advantages and his relatively race-blind milieu of pop culture deprive him of the claim that black characters, from the slave narratives on, traditionally exert upon the American conscience: the heroism that persecution and disadvantage impose." Of course, that is horrifically racist. How something so stupidly racist was allowed to run in the *New Yorker* still stuns me all these years later. The question that I'm interested in, though, is had Whitehead made his character more Black, whatever that means, would Updike have considered it more political? Does the character have to be stereotypical for the novel to be considered identity-based political fiction? If an African American author writes a novel that illustrates what Updike wants of all Black novels, a heroic fight against persecution and disadvantage, is she writing a political novel, and not so if not?

In another *New Yorker* review, John Updike praised *The Spell* by the gay writer Alan Hollinghurst. Updike loved the novel, but then, as was his wont, he added another wounding dig. He claimed to be not totally invested in the characters' relationships because they somehow seemed less interesting than straight ones. There was more at stake in heterosexual relationships because the sex could possibly lead to reproduction. Think about that. If you can't have biological children by having intercourse, your relationship isn't that meaningful. Is a novel about gay love identity-based political fiction?

We know that Updike's novels aren't considered identity-based political fiction. Does a white man behaving as a white man should make a work not political? Does a straight man having sex with a woman and her, oh my god, getting pregnant mean that the novel isn't identity based?

What is going on here?

To find out, let's talk about the greatest of art—its highest form—the Marvel Cinematic Universe.

When the comics made the new Thor a woman instead of choosing to repeat the familiar hunky blond man trope, the fandom exploded with vitriolic rebellion. This could not be, we won't accept this, and so forth. The dominant theme of the responses was that Thor had become political. When Thor was male, it wasn't political, but when she's female, it is.

That a Pakistani Muslim Ms. Marvel is political goes without saying.

But my favorite uproar is about Captain America going Black. When, after the comic and comical death of the original, Marvel made an African American man Captain America, many fans went insane. And of course one of the first responses was "Why would you turn Captain America political?" When a character with a name like Captain America is created to fight the Nazis, created to help recruit young men and women into the armed forces, to defend the values of the country bearing his name—when that character is a white man, it's not political. But when he's Black, obviously it is.

I will not mention the fact that the new Superman, son of the old Superman, is gay or discuss the reaction, because—well because that's DC and not Marvel.

Now, obviously, denigrating works by calling them political rankles me. Dismissing writers for being political seems similar to me to telling LeBron James that he should shut up and stick to basketball. When Thomas Mallon and Pamela Paul suggest that it's wonderful that Franzen avoids politics, they are in essence telling the rest of us to shut up and stick to novels about couples divorcing in Minneapolis. I know that this is my issue—and boy, do I have issues—but there's a constant nagging in the back of my head. I hear Daddy and Mommy telling the kids to play with these dolls here and not disturb them while they stomp on everyone else and crush the world, for the benefit of the kids, of course. Mommy and Daddy can exterminate entire populations overseas, can raise money by, say, incarcerating 10 percent of the population, basically do whatever they want, and you kids must play in this little corner here.

Writers are essentially being admonished to stay in our lanes, to avoid writing about anything that might upset the status quo.

A few months ago, I read that a state senator in Texas had drawn up a list of 850 books that "could make students feel discomfort" and was demanding that school districts across the state report whether any of these books were in their classrooms or libraries. Whenever I come across something like this, my first reaction is to assume it is satire. It takes me a minute to realize it's not. This senator wants to make sure that students do not read any books that could cause them "guilt, anguish, or any other form of psychological distress because of their race or sex." I don't care whether such impulses come from the right or the left, but the idea that a book is not supposed to cause any psychological distress is hogwash. To put it mildly, if a book doesn't make me feel discomfort, why even bother? For crying out loud, even bad romance novels should cause some discomfort. Will he commit, or won't he? Is she going to pick the right one or the wrong one?

Literature is never safe, and great literature is threatening, whether that threat is conscious or not.

I hate this categorization of novels into political or not. I divide novels into two categories: Good novels and bad novels.

COMFORTING MYTHS

I get tired of hearing people say they hate political novels after reading a bad one.

With few exceptions, a novel is bad if it's heavy-handed, if it is about one agenda and little else, whether that agenda is political or not.

With few exceptions, a novel is good, or can be, if it has many threads and is about many things, most of them undefinable.

I get tired of hearing writers talk about how identity politics is either hurting literature or reviving it. Identity-based political novels have been around for as long as the novel has. It is neither good nor bad in and of itself. It's bad when it's bad, good when it's good.

I'm tired of readers saying that nonpolitical fiction is more universal. That's wrong by definition. Something is either universal or not. It can't be more so. Something can't be universal if it affects only you and your neighbors, if it's only you and your suburban development. The dominant culture always likes to think of itself as universal. It isn't.

I was told recently that when interviewers asked

the great Toni Morrison whether her work was universal, she replied that it wasn't. She considered her work to be grounded in African American traditions. I agree with her. Jonathan Franzen's work is grounded in white European traditions. Neither is exactly universal. And they are both political. Saying that some of us can enjoy a novel, and learn from it, doesn't make it universal.

I'm tired of listening to writers try to explain that one writer—let's say Cheever or Munro—deals with issues that are universal whereas James Baldwin is more political, or more dated, or more fill in the blank. What fiction is universal? I can just imagine going up to a prisoner being tortured in Abu Ghraib and saying, "Here, read this short story by John Cheever, which every human on earth can identify with."

There are seven billion people on this earth and almost none of them have read Updike. What's universal? What percentage of the seven billion have read Proust, Baldwin, what have you? Universal has no meaning, sort of like political.

COMFORTING MYTHS

So yes, it rankles me when something is arbitrarily considered less than another because we deem it political. When the *New Yorker* in its issue right after September 11 asked various writers to elaborate on their experiences and reactions to the disaster, almost all waxed lyrical about the national grief, the greatness of New York, the irrepressible American spirit. Susan Sontag, glorious Sontag, began her piece with the following: "Let's by all means grieve together. But let's not be stupid together." God, I love her. She then went ahead and, as we say, called it what it is, called the bullshit bullshit, telling us in no uncertain terms to take the blinders off. She was pilloried by everyone for it. Nowadays, you hear a lot of people say how amazing that piece was, but at the time any support for it was muffled by the uproar of anger against her. And of course, many of the responses were, "How dare she bring politics into this?"

As if politics can possibly be excluded from such an act.

CONCERNING THE POLITICAL IN ART

One of the many pearls that stands out for me from that piece by Susan Sontag is this. She wrote, "A lot of thinking needs to be done, and perhaps is being done in Washington and elsewhere, about the ineptitude of American intelligence and counter-intelligence, about options available to American foreign policy, particularly in the Middle East, and about what constitutes a smart program of military defense. But the public is not being asked to bear much of the burden of reality."

Let me repeat the last sentence.

The public is not being asked to bear much of the burden of reality.

I'll ask this here, just pose the question: Does the public consider a work to be political when that work—that novel, poem, painting—asks the public to bear the burden of reality?

Would reality make the public feel discomfort?

A great novel is almost always political because one of its many concerns is political, if we are honest about what we mean by political. For those of us on the periphery of the dominant culture, the political messages might be more urgent because there's more at stake, but they aren't necessarily any less subtle, or any less integrated in the main theme than in novels written by writers who fit more easily into the culture. No matter what Updike says.

Most novels, if not all, are political. You just have to consider whether they are good novels or bad.

I will end with a poem by a wonderful young poet I love: "The Last Analysis; or, I Woke Up," by Jameson Fitzpatrick.

The Last Analysis; or, I Woke Up

and it was political.
I made coffee and the coffee was political.
I took a shower and the water was.
I walked down the street in short shorts and a Bob Mizer
    tank top
and they were political, the walking and the shorts and the
    beefcake

CONCERNING THE POLITICAL IN ART

silkscreen of the man posing in a G-string. I forgot my
   sunglasses
and later, on the train, that was political,
when I studied every handsome man in the car.
Who I thought was handsome was political.
I went to work at the university and everything was
very obviously political, the department and the institution.
All the cigarettes I smoked between classes were political,
where I threw them when I was through.
I was blond and it was political.
So was the difference between "blond" and "blonde."
I had long hair and it was political. I shaved my head and it
   was.
That I didn't know how to grieve when another person was
   killed in America
was political, and it was political when America killed
   another person,
who they were and what color and gender and who I am in
   relation.
I couldn't think about it for too long without feeling a
   helplessness
like childhood. I was a child and it was political, being a boy
who was bad at it. I couldn't catch and so the ball became
   political.
My mother read to me almost every night
and the conditions that enabled her to do so were political.

COMFORTING MYTHS

That my father's money was new was political, that it was
 proving something.
Someone called me faggot and it was political.
I called myself a faggot and it was political.
How difficult my life felt relative to how difficult it was
was political. I thought I could become a writer
and it was political that I could imagine it.
I thought I was not a political poet and still
my imagination was political.
It had been, this whole time I was asleep.

"The Last Analysis; or, I Woke Up" is reprinted by permission of the author.

COMFORTING MYTHS

NOTES FROM A PURVEYOR

Before he died, my father reminded me that when I was four and he asked what I wanted to be when I grew up, I said I wanted to be a writer. Of course, what I meant by "writer" then was a writer of Superman comics. In part I was infatuated with the practically invulnerable Man of Steel, his blue eyes and his spit curl. I wanted both to be him and to marry him—to be his Robin, so to speak. But more important, I wanted to write his story, the adventures of the man who fought for truth, justice, and the American Way—if only I could figure out what the fuck the American Way was.

How could I tell the story with such glaring holes in my knowledge? I was terribly bothered that I did not know what the American Way was, and became even more so when I began to wonder whether there was such a thing as the Lebanese Way and whether I would recognize it. My parents were Lebanese, but I was born in Jordan, raised in Kuwait. Could my way be Kuwaiti and not Lebanese? Since most of my classmates were Palestinians, I had a Ramallah accent. Did that mean I'd lost my way?

I wanted to tell stories that belonged to me. Superman would be my friend, his world mine. In a single bound, he would leap the tallest buildings, basically my house and my cousins' across the street. My Superman would be more powerful than a locomotive, stronger than my father's red Rambler. I wished to share my story with the world, and it did not occur to me at that age to ask whether the world had any interest.

COMFORTING MYTHS

Who gets to tell stories? Let me answer this quickly: For the most part—and the exceptions are relatively recent—the writers who are allowed to talk are those who prop up the dominant culture, who reflect it with a gilded mirror. But wait: writers have been critical of the dominant culture for quite a while, you may say. Look at James Baldwin, look at Margaret Atwood and *The Handmaid's Tale.* Well, fine, but criticism of the culture is not necessarily a threat to it. When the story is truly threatening, the writer is marginalized, either deemed a "political" writer or put in a box to be safely celebrated as some sort of "minority" writer. In his day Baldwin was considered more a Black writer than a writer, and so he still is. If he is inching his way into the canon, it is because the culture has shifted. Overt racism is a bad thing now, so a liberal American can read *Another Country* and think, sure, there were a few bad apples back then, but this is not about me or how I live. It is easier now to tell ourselves that Baldwin is not talking about us, that he is criticizing people we no longer are.

When I bring this up in conversation, people stop me in my tracks because, you know, Conrad, *Heart of Darkness* and all that. Didn't he criticize empire?

He didn't. A story about a bickering couple does not threaten the institution of marriage. *Heart of Darkness* might disapprove of colonialism, but it's not an attack on empire itself. The book deals in strict dualities and reinforces the superiority of Western culture and ideas. Africa, its jungle, is what blackens Kurtz's heart, and just in case you start to feel uncomfortable because you find yourself identifying with him, the supposed bad apple—the Lynndie England of nineteenth-century Europe—Marlow, the novel's cordon sanitaire, is there to make you feel better. If that's not enough, it's actually some other shadowy narrator telling you what he heard when listening to Marlow's story, so you, imperial citizen, are at least two steps removed from the apple and its African rot. No need for you to feel yourself in jeopardy. Your world might not be perfect, but that other world, that world of the other, is just simply horrid.

In Chinua Achebe's 1977 essay on *Heart of Darkness*, he accuses Conrad of "thoroughgoing" racism and adds, "That this simple truth is glossed over in criticisms of his work is due to the fact that white racism against Africa is such a normal way of thinking that its manifestations go completely unremarked." In other words, Conrad not only shares the dominant point of view but makes it stronger. He might prick it with a pin every now and then, but he is by no means threatening the culture. In fact, he is glorifying it. Achebe uses a phrase that I will return to: "Conrad is a purveyor of comforting myths."

Where I disagree with Achebe is that, because of the racism in *Heart of Darkness*, he refuses to consider it a masterwork. Like all books, Conrad's novel is limited by his vision, his biases, his worldview. There is no writer with limitless vision, no writer whose worldview is shared by everyone. The problem is not that people read *Heart of Darkness* as a masterpiece—it is one—it's that few read books unsanctioned by empire, and even if you wanted to, there aren't that many available. Today's imperial censorship is usually masked as the publisher's bottom line. "This won't sell" is the widest moat in the castle's defenses.

Heart of Darkness echoes everywhere today. Take the American war novels about Vietnam, Afghanistan, Iraq. They are often considered critical of war, hence you might think of them as dangerous to the institution of war. But most of them deal with the suffering of the American soldiers, the Marines who were forced to massacre a village, the pilots who dropped barrel bombs and came home suffering from PTSD. If anything, this is helpful to the cannibalistic war machine. Such war novels make us feel bad and at the same time allow us to see ourselves as the good guys. We are not all terrible, for we suffer too.

In one of the most gorgeous passages at the end of *Heart of Darkness,* Conrad describes at length the suffering of a mass murderer's widow, though he glossed over that of the murderer's victims. Conrad did not create the original mold for this kind of writing—from Homer to Shakespeare to Kipling, many have done it—but he became the standard because he was so good. We invade your countries, destroy your economies, demolish your infrastructures, murder hundreds of thousands of your citizens, and a decade or so later we write beautifully restrained novels about how killing you made us cry.

Among the many writers who have responded to *Heart of Darkness,* my favorite is Tayeb Salih in *Season of Migration to the North.* This short novel, published in Arabic in 1966 (the first English translation came out in 1969), refers to a number of classic works of Western literature—*Othello, The Tempest*—but primarily it engages with Conrad. Where Conrad wrote of colonialism as a misadventure that forced enlightened man to encounter his opposite in the heart of darkness that is Africa, Salih, who is Sudanese, calls the entire enterprise of empire a "deadly disease" that began "a thousand years ago," a contagion that began with the earliest contact, the Crusades. Conrad's Kurtz is mirrored in Salih's Mustafa Sa'eed, who leaves his small Sudanese village and moves to his heart of darkness, London. Once enmeshed in the city's web, Sa'eed decides he will "liberate Africa with his penis." Like Kurtz's time in Africa, Sa'eed's stay in London results in a trail of dead bodies—his lovers who commit suicide, the wife he murders.

Salih's novel simultaneously emphasizes and breaks down the dualities between self and other, between white and black. Sa'eed is shown as both the other and the double of the unnamed narrator, a man from the same village. The line demarcating the dualities is not clear-cut. Compared with *Heart of Darkness, Season of Migration to the North* is a study in subtlety. Whereas the denizens of Conrad's Africa are "just limbs or rolling eyes" who grunt and snort or are cannibals who want to "eat 'im," Salih's Africans think, act, and speak—an amazing concept. And Salih is more generous than Conrad: he allows the denizens of his heart of darkness to be human as well. Even these imperial interlopers are allowed to talk, if only to act on ridiculously sexist and racist sentiments, as with a woman who says to Sa'eed, "Ravish me, you African demon. Burn me in the fire of your temple, you black god. Let me twist and turn in your wild and impassioned rites." (There are prejudices and there are prejudices, of course, and suffering under someone else's does not inoculate you from subjecting others to your own. In Salih's book, in other words, sexism "is such a normal way of thinking that its manifestations go completely unremarked.")

The gravitas in Salih's novel is in the return home. Conrad's Kurtz dies, Marlow returns to England a tad traumatized. In *Season of Migration*, both Sa'eed and the narrator return to Sudan after a stint in London, and they find that they no longer fit where they belong. The narrator says, "By the standards of the European industrial world, we are poor peasants, but when I embrace my grandfather I experience a sense of richness as though I am a note in the heartbeats of the very universe." Neither man can be that note any longer; neither can recover the experience of being part of the village. They are caught in countercurrents.

The novel ends with the narrator in the river, not the Thames or the Congo but the Nile, struggling to stay afloat: "Turning to left and right, I found I was halfway between north and south. I was unable to continue, unable to return. Like a comic actor shouting on a stage, I screamed with all my remaining strength, 'Help! Help!'"

Think "The horror! The horror!"

Colonialism dislocates you in your own home.

I don't have to tell you that Tayeb Salih is not widely read in our dominant culture; or, to put it in the terms I'm using, he isn't allowed to talk here. He isn't a purveyor of *our* comforting myths. He is, however, read among Arabs, at least among the intelligentsia. The book was published to great acclaim and is now recognized as one of the masterpieces of Arabic literature. So: Is Salih the purveyor of comforting myths in *that* world? His novel might not subscribe to the American Way or the Colonialist Way, but does it subscribe to the Arab or the African Way? One has to wonder if it fits into a dominant Arab culture that blames all its ills on colonialism.

The question is important for me, so let me take it a little further: Even though Salih wrote the book in Arabic, he was still a Western-educated man who spent most of his life in London. To the Sudanese, he may be closer than an Englishman, but he isn't exactly one of them, and of course few actual Englishmen would consider him one of their own. He is seen by both sides as the other. Even though his work might sound foreign to most Western readers, his foreignness is the tip of the iceberg, that humongous iceberg of the *other*. Or, if there is such a thing as an otherness scale, then Salih falls at a point along this scale, but not at the far end, and maybe a lot closer than you think.

No matter how bleak things look these days, what with Trump and other racists yelling on the airwaves and committing overt acts of violence, we are living in a time of greater inclusivity than any other. More people are being allowed into the dominant culture, more people are being allowed to talk—maybe not all at the same volume, and there are still not enough voices, but things are quite a bit better than when Salih and Baldwin wrote their novels, and that is reflected in our literature. Every year, novels by women, African Americans, Latinos, queers, by all kinds of "others," are released alongside the white-male-authored books. We have novels by Somalis, Filipinos, Chinese, Indians, Peruvians, Nepalis, you name it.

World literature is now a genre. And as you might have guessed, I have a problem with this.

Let's take an example: Which Chinese writer gets to talk? Amy Tan was born and raised in California and still lives there, so at times she's a Chinese-American writer. Yiyun Li lives in the United States and received her graduate education here, but she was born in China; she's definitely classified as a Chinese writer. They both write in English. Ma Jian lives in London but writes in Chinese. Mo Yan is Chinese, lives in China. He has been accused by the West of not being sufficiently antigovernment, which basically means he does not get to speak for the Chinese. Liu Xiaobo was born and raised and jailed in China, but he was a critic and academic, and who reads that?

It might be fun to play Who Is More Chinese?, but that's not the point here. This isn't about good or bad. I love the work of all the writers I mentioned above. What I'm interested in is who gets to talk. Arguably, Tan and Li are the only "Chinese" who are allowed to talk, who are allowed to tell the story in the United States. There might be one or two others. This is still very limiting, not just in terms of how few are permitted to speak but how the writers are perceived. We're adding another modifier, creating another box—Black writer, queer writer, and now the world literature writer.

On the back cover of one of my novels, I am called "one of world literature's most celebrated voices." (I have a voice, I get to talk, though I often have the impression that I'm supposed to do it sotto voce.) If we look at the impressive list of writers who are part of this world literature thing, we see Tan and Li, Aleksandar Hemon representing Bosnia, Junot Díaz representing the Dominican Republic, Chimamanda Ngozi Adichie and Teju Cole representing Nigeria, Hisham Matar for Libya, Daniel Alarcón for Peru, Salman Rushdie for India, or is it Pakistan—oh, what the hell, let's give him the entire subcontinent. I get Lebanon.

The thing is that we are all Westerners, if not exclusively American. We have all been indoctrinated with a Western education. We can cite Shakespeare with the best of them.

A number of years ago I was a juror for the Neustadt International Prize for Literature, an award sponsored by the University of Oklahoma and the magazine *World Literature Today*. Since this is an international prize, the jury is always composed of international writers. There were jurors representing Lebanon, Mexico, Egypt, Nepal, Palestine, South Africa, Ukraine, the Philippines, and Italy. Only the Italian actually lived in Italy. The rest of us were primarily Americans, living in the United States, almost all associated with American universities. The Mexican was a Texan, the Egyp-

COMFORTING MYTHS

tian a New Yorker; the Nepali taught at Ohio State. Every interview I did as a juror included questions about peace in the Middle East and whether we can achieve it in my lifetime, what it is like in Beirut, and whether I found the trip to Oklahoma tiring. Norman is a four-hour flight from San Francisco. (And while we're talking about universities: MFA programs are a kind of indoctrination too. Certain stories, certain types of stories, and certain ways of telling stories are made more valid than others, and this can be dangerous. From the Congo to the Punjab, if you go to Iowa, you will be learning the Iowa Way. You risk becoming a purveyor of comforting myths.)

This is not a discussion of authenticity. I'm not sure I believe in the concept, particularly in literature. Think of Michael Ondaatje's *The English Patient*, a fully imagined novel with four "other" characters set in "other" locations. Nabokov did not have to be a pedophile to write *Lolita*. After all, art and artifice are related. What I'm talking about, in my roundabout way, is representation—how those of us who fall outside the dominant culture are allowed to speak as the other, and more importantly, for the other.

This is not to say that we were not, or are not, "world literature." We might be different from what passes for regular American lit, or as I like to call it, common literature. What I'm saying is that there is more other, scarier other, translated other, untranslatable other, the utterly strange other, the other who can't stand you. Those of us allowed to speak are the just a tiny drop in a humongous bucket. We are the cute other.

I use the term jokingly, but also deliberately. All of us on that world literature list are basically safe, domesticated, just exotic enough to make our readers feel that they are liberal, not parochial or biased. That is, we are purveyors of comforting myths for a small segment of the dominant culture that would like to see itself as open-minded. I don't mean that as an insult—I love to be read; we all do—but we are serving a purpose that we might not be thinking much about.

COMFORTING MYTHS

In a *New York Times* review, one of my novels was called a "bridge to the Arab soul." I find this phrase discomfiting, mostly because of the words "the Arab," and "soul." Is the Arab soul like the American Way? Do Arabs have just one soul, and if so, can someone please tell me how to find it? "Bridge" I understood. You see, my novel was seen not as American but as representing the Arab world. My novel is a bridge to the world of otherness. I get to talk because I am the bridge. No one on the other side of the bridge gets to. And truly, who would want to cross that bridge and touch the heart of darkness, be soiled by that dark other?

We get to talk because we are seen as the nice tour guides. We can hold the hands of readers of the empire as we travel a short distance onto the bridge and get a glimpse of what's across it, maybe even wave at the poor sods on the other side. We make readers feel good about themselves for delving into our books because they believe they are open-minded about the other. We are purveyors of comforting myths.

Now, again, I want to be read. I love holding

hands. If there is such a bridge, I'd love to take readers for a stroll along it. I doubt any writer feels differently. What I want is to allow other writers to talk, all kinds of writers, or should I say, more others, more-other others.

The problem today is that this culture we live in is lovely and insidious, able, unlike any that has come before it, to integrate criticism of itself and turn it around faster than Klee's Angelus Novus can blink. The culture co-opts others, co-opts their culture, makes us cute and cuddly and lovable, but we never integrate fully.

Every group needs to have an other. I don't know how a society can exist without classifying another as the other. The question for the writers who are getting to talk is where we stand. Inside, outside, in the middle? For so-called world literature writers, it's a troubling question.

You might think this is diversity, but it seems more like homogenization. Sometimes, not always, when I read a novel presented or marketed as "foreign," I feel that I'm reading that common thing, a generic novel hidden behind an alluring facade, a comfortable and familiar book with a sprinkling of exoticness. The names of foods are italicized. Instead of visiting Beijing, I end up at its airport with the same bright Prada and Starbucks stores, maybe one dumpling stand in the corner.

And sometimes even that little stand is troublesome. When I wrote a novel about a reclusive woman who bucks society's rules by having a rich inner life filled with books and art, I was surprised by how many readers identified with her, and more so that many considered her a tragic figure because she lived in a country that had no respect for women. You know: we live in an exceptional country, it's only over there where they ostracize women who refuse to conform. (Our world might not be perfect, but that other world, that world of the other is just simply horrid.)

How to get out of this cycle? I don't know. I'm a writer; answers are not my forte. Complaining certainly is. Moreover, as I have already stated, I'm a writer with a limited view. Like many writers, when

COMFORTING MYTHS

I begin a novel, almost all I worry about is making the damn thing work. I move from one sentence to the next, from one section to another, wondering how and whether everything will fit. I try, however, to write in opposition. By that I mean that whenever a consensus is reached about what constitutes good writing, I instinctively wish to oppose it. When I started writing my first novel, a friend suggested I read John Gardner's *The Art of Fiction*, which allegedly explained the principles of good writing. I hated it, not because it was bad advice but because it felt so limiting. Writers are supposed to show, not tell? I wrote a novel where the protagonist does nothing but tell. A short story should lead to an epiphany? Who needs that? When I'm told I should write a certain way, I bristle. I even attempt to write in opposition to the most recent book I finished. If my previous novel was expansive, I begin to write microscopically; if quiet, I write loudly. It is my nature. I don't know whether this childish rebelliousness helps keep my work "foreign." Most days, I doubt it. I write a book thinking it is subversive, that it might not be a comforting myth, and if it gets read, if I'm lucky, the dominant culture co-opts it like Goya's Saturn devouring his son.

I might think of myself as living in opposition to empire, or I might insist that I write differently from everyone else, but I recognize that I believe this to make myself feel better. Whenever I read reviews of my work, I notice that I am still the tour guide. "Look at those cute Arabs. See, not all of them are bad. And the homosexuals are nice too." Which is to say that opposing the dominant culture is like trying to whittle down a mountain by rubbing it with a silk scarf. Yet a writer must. I may not be able to move mountains like Superman, but I have lovely scarves.

Rabih Alameddine delivered a version of this essay as a lecture at Northwestern University in May 2016. It was published in Harper's Magazine *in June 2018. Rights retained by the author.*

AFTERWORD

HE'S ANGRY ABOUT ALL THE RIGHT THINGS

Joumana Khatib

In 2012, as thousands of Syrians fled the violence in their country for neighboring Lebanon, the novelist Rabih Alameddine visited some of the refugee camps to speak with them. He didn't know what would come of it, but he had experience listening to people in extremis—including dying friends during the AIDS epidemic in San Francisco—and he knew the power of the act. At the very least, he thought, he could talk to the kids about soccer.

What he heard was excruciating: stories of families killed, homes destroyed, history eradicated. Distraught, he hid under the duvet at his mother's home in Beirut.

But Alameddine kept trying. At one settlement, an abandoned Pepsi-Cola plant in the coastal city of Sidon, he encountered a woman who was exasperated and tired of repeating her story.

"If I talk to you, will anything change?" she asked. He told her no. She appraised him for a moment, but once she started, he said, she wouldn't stop talking.

"This is when I realized, again, that the service that I was providing was just as an ear," Alameddine said. "There is absolutely not one thing I can do, but not doing *something* is a crime."

His 2021 novel *The Wrong End of the Telescope* is his effort to process his encounters with refugees in Lebanon and, later, Greece. It follows Mina, a Lebanese American doctor, who has come to the island of Lesbos to volunteer at a refugee camp and is woefully unprepared for what she sees.

"The beach was a scene from a disaster movie,

postevent, when the survivors get together and try to make sense of what happened," she observes, watching as shivering children and traumatized adults reach the island by boat. But the worst of what happens at the camps remains off the page. Later, Mina thinks: "Lesbos was a somewhat humane mess when we were there. Shortly thereafter it became an inhumane one."

There is also a personal dimension to her trip. Mina is the closest to Lebanon she's been in years—since her family disowned her and she transitioned genders—and the refugees are her people.

Alameddine, the author of six books in addition to *The Wrong End of the Telescope*, often focuses on Lebanon, upheaval, and the people who go unseen and disregarded in the world. Refugees are particularly invisible, he said. "We step over them."

His 1998 debut, *Koolaids*, leaps from San Francisco during the AIDS epidemic to Beirut during the Lebanese civil war. Alameddine, who is gay, was frustrated by what he saw as cultural amnesia when it came to both crises. "I hated what was passing for gay literature, for AIDS literature," he said. "And forget anything Lebanese."

"He's angry about all the right things," said the author Aleksandar Hemon, a longtime friend. "It is an aspect of his deep involvement and care for the world."

Despite the outrage that can fuel them, Alameddine's books are funny and irreverent. The arts—literature, poetry, paintings—provide an escape for characters in unbearable situations, and classical allusions abound. Humor, sex, and grief collide, often on the same page, and there's plenty of camp: Death, in his 2016 novel *The Angel of History,* appears as a fey, beret-wearing figure with a black manicure who thinks, "Arabs make my life worth living, such pleasure they have given me through the years."

"There are many terrible things about being Lebanese, but to be any kind of storyteller in our part of the world," Alameddine said, "there has to be a lightness of touch."

Born to a Lebanese family in Jordan, Alameddine lived there, then in Kuwait and Lebanon, before his family, sensing the stirrings of the civil war, sent him to England in 1975. He eventually settled in San Francisco, living there for decades.

In California he earned an engineering degree and an MBA—"it never occurred to me to go get an MFA"—tended bar and painted. He helped start a gay soccer team, though by the mid-1990s, half its players had died of AIDS complications.

Alameddine was nearly forty by the time *Koolaids* was released, and at the beginning of his literary career, he was invited to join a writing group with "some really important writers," he recalled.

"I lasted for about four months—they kicked me out," he said. "And we're still friends." (In 2021, he moved cross-country to teach at the University of Virginia's creative writing program.)

Alameddine has never felt "totally accepted, whether in Lebanon or the U.S.," in the gay community or the writer community, he said. "I always get accused by the Lebanese that I'm writing for a Western audience. I get accused by the West that

I'm writing for a Lebanese audience. The truth is, I don't care about either of them."

Hemon, his friend, put it simply: "Each book is a kind of a new homeland for him."

Hamed Sinno, the lead singer of Mashrou' Leila, a popular Lebanese indie-rock band, said that encountering Alameddine's work was a revelation. Alameddine represented "someone from another generation who survived AIDS and lived to write about it, and survived the civil war and lived to write about it," Sinno said.

Alameddine is baffled when readers express surprise he could inhabit the mind of a character who doesn't resemble him. "I was able to write a book where the narrator is a masochist who gets whipped," he said of *The Angel of History.* "My idea of rough sex is sleeping on cotton sheets that are less than 600 count."

His outsider perspective helps him find the "Goldilocks distance" from his subjects. With *Telescope,* he set out to write a novel that encompassed his own experiences and the stories of the refugees he met, but, unable to extricate himself enough, he developed the character of Mina, someone whose life differed from his own.

But he doesn't vanish from the story. An unnamed author scuttles along the margins of the novel, and his inability to write about his volunteer work on Lesbos or to comprehend the crisis is a running theme. (At one point, the author, so overwhelmed by what he's seen on the island, locks himself in his hotel room and blares Mahler.)

Mina herself pokes fun at the writer character. "You once wrote that you felt embarrassed when critics and reviewers classified your work as immigrant literature," Mina says. "You joked that the worst immigration trauma you had endured was when your flight from Heathrow was delayed."

According to Alameddine, that Mina is trans isn't incidental, since "she has had to kill off and bury her past on more than one occasion." At the same time, Susan Stryker, a transgender scholar and a friend of Alameddine's, said it was refreshing to encounter trans characters whose gender identity isn't their overriding storyline.

"Trans people transition gender at some point—

duh. It's one thing we do, but it's not all we do," Stryker said. And seeing characters like Mina in this setting—doing deeply moral, humanitarian work—rejects a stereotype of trans people as "evil deceivers and make-believers," she said.

In some ways, Alameddine said, writing the refugee characters was the easiest part. Mina has an especially close relationship with one family, headed by a woman with advanced liver disease. But dozens of migrants cycle through the novel, from a gay Iraqi couple puzzled by the Syrian families processed before them, to a gaggle of children who charm volunteers into buying an unholy number of chocolate bars.

One chapter, titled "How to Make Liberace Jealous," was inspired by the dwelling of a woman Alameddine met in Lebanon. She had painstakingly decorated her pantry with sequins, with results "so over the top that many a drag queen would kill for it."

"You wondered what kind of person would think it was a good idea to donate thousands of sequins to Syrian refugees who had nothing left, whose entire lives had been extirpated. Bright, shiny, gaudy, useless sequins?" Mina thinks. "A fabulous one, of course, a lovely, most wonderful human being."

From the New York Times*. © 2021 The New York Times Company. All rights reserved. Used under license.*

ACKNOWLEDGMENTS

In spring 2016, I was the Writer in Residence at the Center for the Writing Arts, Northwestern University. "Comforting Myths: Notes from a Purveyor" was a talk I gave there. I wish to thank the Center at Northwestern and the English and creative writing faculty for their support. I would also like to thank Hasan Altaf and the editors of *Harper's* for publishing the talk/essay in the magazine, as well as Rebecca Solnit and Robert Atwan for selecting it for *The Best American Essays 2019*.

ACKNOWLEDGMENTS

In fall 2021, I was the Kapnick Distinguished Writer-in-Residence at the University of Virginia. "Concerning the Political in Art" was a talk I gave there. I wish to thank the Kapnick Foundation and the creative writing faculty for their support (Yay, Micheline!).

I also wish to thank Eric Brandt for publishing this book.

Kapnick Foundation

Distinguished Writer-in-Residence Lectures

Three Talks
Brenda Hillman

The Art of Fiction
James Salter